AMALFI COAST TRAVEL GUIDE 2023

Your Complete Portable Travel Guide to the Amalfi Coast and Beyond, Including the Most Scenic, Secret Landscapes, Art, and Food.

MARIO ROCALLI

Copyright © 2022 [Mario Rocalli],

All Rights Reserved ,this work is protected by copyright law and is provided solely for the use of instructors in teaching their courses and assessing student learning. Any other use, including commercial reuse, sale, or redistribution is prohibited without the express written permission of [Mario Rocalli].

TABLE OF CONTENTS

INTRODUCTION	**9**
Chapter 1: Before you travel	**13**
Best time to travel	13
Best place to stay	17
Book Accommodations	20
Plan Your Itinerary	21
Some Italian phrases	30
Visa requirements :.	31
Chapter 2: Getting Around on Amalfi	**35**
Transportation in Amalfi Coast	35
Chapter 3: Where to Stay	**39**
Luxury hotels	39
Boutique hotel	42
Bed and breakfast	49
Agriturismi	55
Chapter 4: places for sightseeing	**58**
Town	58
Beaches on Amalfi Coast	62
Historic sites of Amalfi	66
Garden in the Amalfi Coast	70
Chapter 5: Food and drinks	**74**
Cafe and Restaurant	81
Chapter 6: outdoor activities	**89**
Hiking	**89**
Scuba diving	92
Kayaking	96

    Paragliding   100

Chapter 7: Shopping Experience   **105**
    Famous Markets   105
    Special Stores   108

Chapter 8: Culture and Arts   **114**
    Festivals   114
    Art Galleries   117
    Music   121

Chapter 9: Practical Information   **127**
    Currency of Amalfi Coast   127
    Safety and Health   129
    Sustainabilit and Responsible tourism   140

Conclusion   **143**

INTRODUCTION

Welcome to the stunning Amalfi Coast, a paradise situated along the gorgeous coastline of southern Italy. As a local of this breathtaking region, I am delighted to be your guide on this journey of exploration.

The Amalfi Coast is a place that captures the hearts and souls of all who have the honor to explore its shores. With its dramatic cliffs plunging into the crystal-clear waters of the Tyrrhenian Sea, it has a natural beauty that is incomparable. This UNESCO World Heritage site is a testament to Mother Nature's artistry, where lush forests, vibrant lemon groves, and colorful bougainvillea create a landscape that looks like a dream.

In addition to its stunning scenery, the Amalfi Coast is steeped in a rich history and culture. Centuries ago, this region was a maritime powerhouse, its cities and towns flourishing as bustling trading ports. The legendary seafaring republic of Amalfi was once a powerful force, playing a major role in the exchange of goods, ideas, and knowledge throughout the Mediterranean.

Today, remnants of that illustrious past can still be felt in the architecture, customs, and hospitality of the locals. Walking through the narrow cobblestone streets of Amalfi, Positano, and other charming villages, you'll be taken back to a bygone era, where medieval watchtowers stand tall, and pastel-colored houses cling to the cliffs like a work of art.

The Amalfi Coast's cultural heritage is equally captivating. From the traditional craftsmanship of ceramics and handmade paper to the lively festivals that fill the air with music and joy, this region is a treasure trove of artistic expression. Whether you're enjoying the melodious notes of classical music at the renowned Ravello Festival or savoring the delicious flavors of local cuisine, each moment is an invitation to immerse yourself in the vibrant soul of the Amalfi Coast.

Throughout this travel guide, I will share with you the hidden gems, the must-visit landmarks, and the lesser-known trails that reveal the true essence of our beloved Amalfi Coast. From the iconic towns of Amalfi and Positano to the tranquil beauty of Capri and the captivating heights of Ravello, we will explore every aspect of this Mediterranean jewel.

So, dear traveler, buckle up and get ready for a breathtaking adventure that will leave a lasting impression on your heart. The Amalfi Coast is ready to welcome you with open arms, ready to enchant, inspire, and create memories that will last a lifetime. Let us embark on this extraordinary voyage together and uncover the magic of the Amalfi Coast, one chapter at a time.

Chapter 1: Before you travel

Best time to travel

As a proud native of the stunning Amalfi Coast, I'm thrilled to share the insider secrets about the ideal time to explore this picturesque region. From the cascades of wisterias and bougainvilleas in spring to the azure waters and golden beaches in summer, the Amalfi Coast is a Mediterranean gem that will leave an indelible mark on your soul. Let me be your guide and paint a vivid picture of the perfect moments to savor this coastal paradise.

Spring Symphony - A Blossoming Wonder April to June is the ideal time to step foot on our terracotta paths and be greeted by a symphony of vibrant colors and fragrances. Witness the beauty of nature's revival as cascades of wisterias, bougainvilleas, and lemon blossoms fill the air with a delightful aroma. Plus, you'll enjoy mild temperatures, fewer crowds, and plenty of festivals.

Summer Serenade - Sun, Sea, and Swaying Palms July to September is when the Amalfi Coast reaches its pinnacle of allure. Immerse yourself in the azure waters, bask in the golden sun-kissed beaches, and indulge in the rhythmic melodies of the Mediterranean waves. Plus, you'll find vibrant beach clubs, lively nightlife, and a festive atmosphere that encapsulates the true essence of the Italian dolce vita.

Autumn's Enchantment - A Painter's Palette October to November is when the Amalfi Coast transforms into a painter's palette, with a kaleidoscope of red, orange, and gold adorning the cliffs and vineyards. As the tourist crowds diminish, you can discover the quieter side of our coastal towns, savor the harvest flavors, and embark on invigorating hiking trails amidst nature's magnificent artwork.

Winter Wonder - A Cozy Coastal Retreat December to February is the ideal time to experience the authentic charm of our towns. Cozy up by crackling fireplaces, sip limoncello to ward off the chill, delve into the region's rich history, explore ancient sites without the hustle, and relish the tranquility of coastal life.

No matter the season you choose to visit, the Amalfi Coast promises an unforgettable journey. Each chapter of the year unveils a unique tapestry of experiences, allowing you to embrace the coastal magic in your own way. So, listen to the rhythm of the locals, heed the whispers of the wind, and embark on an Amalfi Coast adventure that will stay with you forever. Welcome to our world, where time stands still and beauty knows no bounds.

Best place to stay

I'm delighted to guide you through the best places to stay in this enchanting coastal paradise.

Amalfi Town: Nestled in the heart of the coast, Amalfi Town offers a perfect blend of history and seaside allure. Immerse yourself in the vibrant atmosphere of its historic center, adorned with medieval architecture and hidden gems waiting to be discovered. Stay in a boutique hotel overlooking the azure waters, and indulge in the delicious local cuisine while enjoying breathtaking views.

Positano: Prepare to fall in love with Positano, a jewel that cascades down the cliffs in a vibrant mosaic of pastel hues. Choose a cliffside hotel with panoramic terraces, where you can wake up to awe-inspiring vistas of the sea and town. Stroll through its narrow streets lined with fashionable boutiques and enjoy lazy days on its picturesque beaches. Positano is pure magic.

Ravello: Perched high above the coast, Ravello is a serene escape for those seeking tranquility and inspiration. This enchanting hilltop village is home to stunning gardens, such as Villa Cimbrone and Villa Rufolo, where you can witness nature's artistry. Stay in a charming villa or a boutique hotel, and savor the harmonious melodies of the annual Ravello Festival.

Sorrento: Known as the gateway to the Amalfi Coast, Sorrento offers a captivating blend of history, culture, and breathtaking views. Choose a hotel overlooking the Bay of Naples and Mount Vesuvius, and explore the town's ancient alleys and bustling Piazza Tasso. Sorrento serves as an ideal base for day trips to Pompeii, Capri, and other nearby destinations.

Praiano: If you seek a quieter retreat without compromising on beauty, Praiano is your haven. With its charming village atmosphere and stunning vistas, this coastal gem offers a more laid-back experience. Choose a cliffside hotel with private terraces, where you can bask in the golden hues of sunset while enjoying the tranquility of the sea.

Maiori: For those seeking a more relaxed beach experience, Maiori beckons with its long stretch of golden sands. Stay in one of the beachfront hotels, where you can wake up to the sound of gentle waves and spend lazy days under the warm Mediterranean sun. Explore the town's vibrant promenade and indulge in the delightful local cuisine.

No matter where you choose to stay along the Amalfi Coast, you'll be greeted with warm hospitality, captivating scenery, and a sense of timeless beauty. Each place has its unique charm, allowing you to create unforgettable memories.

Book Accommodations

Booking your accommodation before visiting Amalfi Coast to ensure a stress free and enjoyable trip . It is very important to start with researching the different towns and villages in the region and identify which one will suit you perfectly. After you have made your decisions, look for accommodation options in the vicinity that match your budget such as hostels, bed, breakfast, or apartments. Pay attention to amenities offered such as wi-fi, air conditioning and parking. Check if the property is located near restaurant shops and transportations as this can greatly enhance your experience.

Plan Your Itinerary

The Amalfi Coast is a breathtakingly beautiful destination in Italy that offers stunning coastal views, charming towns, and a rich cultural heritage. Planning your itinerary for a trip to the Amalfi Coast requires careful consideration to make the most of your time and experience everything this enchanting region has to offer. Here is a wonderful summary to help you plan your perfect Amalfi Coast travel guide.

Determine the Duration of Your Trip: Start by deciding how long you want to spend exploring the Amalfi Coast. While it's possible to see the highlights in a few days, it's recommended to allocate at least a week to fully immerse yourself in the region's beauty.

Choose the Best Time to Visit: The ideal time to visit the Amalfi Coast is during the shoulder seasons of spring (April to June) and fall (September to October) when it's nice outside and there aren't as many people around Avoiding the peak summer months will ensure a more peaceful and enjoyable experience.

Select Your Base: The Amalfi Coast is dotted with several charming towns, and choosing a base for your stay is crucial. Popular options include Sorrento, Positano, Amalfi, and Ravello. Each town has its unique charm, so consider your preferences, budget, and proximity to attractions when making your decision.

Explore the Coastal Towns: Dedicate time to visit the picturesque coastal towns along the Amalfi Coast. Positano is famous for its colorful cliffside houses, while Amalfi boasts a stunning cathedral and a vibrant waterfront. Ravello offers breathtaking views from its mountaintop location, and Sorrento serves as a gateway to the region with its lively atmosphere and access to nearby attractions.

Discover Hidden Gems: While the popular towns are a must-visit, don't forget to explore some lesser-known gems. Visit the enchanting village of Atrani, with its narrow streets and charming atmosphere.

Take a boat trip to the beautiful island of Capri and explore its stunning Blue Grotto. Discover the ancient ruins of Pompeii and Herculaneum for a glimpse into the region's rich history.

Hike the Path of the Gods: Lace up your hiking boots and embark on the famous Path of the Gods (Sentiero degli Dei). This spectacular trail offers awe-inspiring views of the coast, lush landscapes, and an opportunity to immerse yourself in nature. The trail can be accessed from various points, including Bomerano and Nocelle.

Savor the Local Cuisine: Indulge in the delightful culinary offerings of the Amalfi Coast. Sample the region's famous limoncello, fresh seafood, and traditional dishes like spaghetti alle vongole (spaghetti with clams) and sfogliatella (a local pastry). Visit local markets and family-run trattorias to experience authentic flavors and warm hospitality.

Relax on the Beaches: The Amalfi Coast is renowned for its stunning beaches and crystal-clear waters. Spend a day lounging on the sun-soaked beaches of Positano, Amalfi, or Maiori. Alternatively, take a boat trip along the coast to discover hidden coves and secluded spots for a peaceful escape.

Plan Transportation: The Amalfi Coast is well-connected by various transportation options. Consider renting a car for flexibility, but be aware that the narrow roads and parking challenges can be daunting. Alternatively, utilize public transportation, including buses and ferries, to explore the region conveniently and enjoy the scenic routes.

Embrace the Slow Pace: Finally, remember to embrace the slow pace and relaxed atmosphere of the Amalfi Coast. Take leisurely strolls, soak in the panoramic views, and immerse yourself in the local culture.

Plan for Flexibility: While it's essential to have a rough itinerary, be open to spontaneity and unexpected discoveries. Leave room in your schedule for impromptu stops, hidden viewpoints, and local recommendations. Some of the best experiences can happen when you allow yourself to wander and follow your instincts.

Prioritize Must-See Attractions: Make a list of the must-see attractions and experiences that you don't want to miss. Whether it's visiting the iconic Duomo di Amalfi, exploring the gardens of Villa Cimbrone in Ravello, or witnessing a stunning sunset from the cliffs of Positano, ensure these highlights are included in your itinerary.

Consider Day Trips: The Amalfi Coast is perfectly situated for day trips to nearby destinations. Explore the ruins of Pompeii, a city frozen in time by the eruption of Mount Vesuvius. Visit the ancient city of Paestum, famous for its well-preserved Greek temples. Take a boat trip to the enchanting island of Ischia or venture inland to the picturesque town of Sorrento.

Plan for Relaxation: Amidst all the sightseeing and exploration, remember to allocate time for relaxation and rejuvenation. Take advantage of the region's luxurious spas, indulge in a leisurely day at a beach club, or simply find a cozy spot with a stunning view to unwind and soak in the peaceful ambiance.

Capture the Memories: The Amalfi Coast is a photographer's paradise, so be sure to capture the memories. Whether you're using a professional camera or your smartphone, take the time to frame the stunning landscapes, vibrant streets, and colorful facades. Create lasting memories of your journey along this picturesque coastline.

Be Mindful of Seasonal Events: Check if there are any local festivals, events, or cultural celebrations happening during your visit. These occasions provide an opportunity to witness traditional music, dance, and culinary delights, offering a deeper understanding of the local culture and traditions.

Pack Smart: When packing for your Amalfi Coast adventure, consider the weather and activities you plan to engage in. Pack comfortable walking shoes, light and breathable clothing for the warm Mediterranean climate, sunscreen, a hat, and a reusable water bottle for staying hydrated during your explorations.

Learn Basic Italian Phrases: While English is spoken in tourist areas, learning a few basic Italian phrases will go a long way in connecting with locals and showing respect for their culture. Simple greetings, thank you, and please will be appreciated and can open doors to engaging conversations and memorable interactions.

Embrace the Magic of the Nights: The Amalfi Coast takes on a magical ambiance at night. Take evening walks along the promenades, dine at romantic seaside restaurants, and embrace the romance of the illuminated coastal towns. Allow yourself to be captivated by the twinkling lights and the soothing sound of the waves.

Immerse Yourself in the Local Vibe: Finally, as you plan your itinerary, keep in mind that the true essence of the Amalfi Coast lies in its people, culture, and way of life. Interact with the locals, embrace their warmth and hospitality, and immerse yourself in the vibrant local vibe that makes this destination truly special.

Some Italian phrases

Here are some of the most critical Italian phrases that you should know:

Ciao! - Hello! Goodbye!

Buongiorno! - Good morning!

Buon pomeriggio! - Good afternoon!

Buona sera! - Good evening!

Come sta? - How are you?

Sto Bene - I'm fine

Per favore - Please

Grazie - Thank you

Prego - You're welcome

Mi dispiace - I'm sorry

Arrivederci - Goodbye

Posso avere...? - Can I have...?

Quanto costa? - How much does it cost?

Non capisco - I don't understand

Parla inglese? - Do you speak English?

Visa requirements

: Visa requirements for the Amalfi Coast depend on your nationality and the duration of your stay. Here is a wonderful summary to help you understand the visa requirements for traveling to the Amalfi Coast.

Schengen Area: The Amalfi Coast is located in Italy, which is a member of the Schengen Area. If you are a citizen of a country that is also a member of the Schengen Area, such as the United States, Canada, Australia, or many European countries, you can enter Italy and the Amalfi Coast for tourism purposes without a visa and stay for up to 90 days within a 180-day period.

Non-Schengen Area: If you are a citizen of a country that is not a member of the Schengen Area, you may need to apply for a Schengen visa before traveling to the Amalfi Coast. Check with the Italian embassy or consulate in your home country to determine the specific visa requirements and application process. It's advisable to apply for the visa well in advance of your planned travel dates.

Visa Exemptions: Some nationalities are exempt from the Schengen visa requirement for short stays. For example, citizens of certain countries, such as the United States, Canada, Australia, and New Zealand, can enter Italy and the Schengen Area for tourism or business purposes for up to 90 days without a visa. However, it's important to note that these exemptions may have certain conditions and limitations, so it's always best to check with the relevant authorities for the most up-to-date information.

Long-Term Stays: If you plan to stay on the Amalfi Coast for more than 90 days or for purposes other than tourism, such as studying or working, you may need to submit an application for a different kind of visa, such as a work or student visa. In such cases, you should contact the Italian embassy or consulate in your home country or the relevant authorities in Italy to obtain the necessary visa and permit.

Passport Validity: Ensure that your passport is valid for at least six months beyond your planned departure date from Italy. This is a general requirement for most countries and will help avoid any issues during your travel.

Travel Insurance: It's highly recommended to have travel insurance that covers medical expenses and provides adequate coverage for the duration of your stay in the Amalfi Coast. While not a visa requirement, having travel insurance is important for your peace of mind and to handle any unexpected situations that may arise during your trip.

Remember to always check the official websites of the Italian embassy or consulate in your home country for the most accurate and up-to-date information regarding visa requirements for the Amalfi Coast. It's essential to plan ahead and ensure you have the necessary visas or exemptions in place to enjoy a smooth and hassle-free journey to this stunning destination.

Chapter 2: Getting Around on Amalfi Coast

Transportation in Amalfi Coast

The Amalfi Coast is renowned for its stunning beauty and picturesque towns, and exploring this captivating region is made easy with a variety of transportation options. From ferries and buses to car rentals, there are numerous ways to navigate the Amalfi Coast and connect to its charming towns.

Ferries and Boats:

Ferries and boats are a popular choice for exploring the Amalfi Coast, offering breathtaking views of the coastline from the water. From the main ports of Sorrento, Naples, and Salerno, you can catch regular ferry services to towns such as Amalfi, Positano, and Capri. These services provide a convenient and scenic way to travel between the towns, allowing you to appreciate the coastline's splendor from a different perspective.

Buses:

The SITA buses are the primary mode of public transportation along the Amalfi Coast. They connect the major towns and offer a reliable and cost-effective way to get around. The buses run frequently and follow the coastal road, winding through the cliffs and providing stunning views along the way. The main bus route runs from Sorrento to Salerno, passing through towns like Positano, Amalfi, and Ravello. Be ready for full buses during the busiest travel season.

Private Transfers and Taxis:

Private transfers and taxis are available for a more comfortable and personalized transportation experience. You can arrange for private drivers or taxis to pick you up from airports, train stations, or hotels and transport you directly to your desired destination. This option offers convenience and flexibility, allowing you to customize your itinerary and travel at your own pace.

Car Rentals:

Renting a car is an excellent option for those who prefer more independence and flexibility while exploring the Amalfi Coast. Having your own vehicle allows you to venture off the beaten path and discover hidden gems at your leisure. However, keep in mind that driving along the narrow, winding roads of the Amalfi Coast can be challenging, especially for inexperienced drivers. It is advisable to choose a small car and consider purchasing comprehensive insurance coverage. Additionally, parking can be limited and expensive in the towns, so it's important to plan ahead and utilize public parking areas.

When it comes to car rentals, there are several reputable companies to choose from. To ensure the best prices and availability, it is advised to reserve your rental car in advance. Some popular car rental companies in the area include Hertz, Avis, Europcar, and Sixt. Be sure to read the terms and conditions, including any restrictions or additional fees, and choose a rental agency with convenient pickup and drop-off locations.

Exploring the Amalfi Coast is an adventure in itself, and the transportation options available provide unique opportunities to immerse yourself in the region's beauty. Whether you choose ferries, buses, private transfers, or car rentals, each mode of transportation offers its own charm and convenience, allowing you to connect to the charming towns and create unforgettable memories along the way.

Chapter 3: Where to Stay

Luxury hotels

As a proud local, I am thrilled to share with you the essence of our beloved region and the unparalleled luxury hotels that make it a dream destination.

When it comes to choosing where to stay on the Amalfi Coast, allow me to guide you towards the epitome of refined elegance. Our luxury hotels are not just places to rest your head; they are exquisite havens that immerse you in a world of opulence and tranquility.

Picture yourself waking up to the gentle caress of the Mediterranean breeze, the sun-kissed cliffs soaring above the azure sea. This is the enchanting setting of Hotel Belmond Caruso, an icon perched on a cliff, offering majestic views that will leave you breathless. From its meticulously designed suites to the infinity pool seemingly merging with the horizon, every detail of your stay at Hotel Belmond Caruso is crafted to elevate your senses.

For those seeking secluded paradise, Monastero Santa Rosa Hotel & Spa is a gem nestled within a 17th-century monastery. Here, history and luxury intertwine, offering meticulously restored architecture, stunning gardens, and views that will transport you to another world. Unwind in this haven of tranquility and indulge in the divine treatments at the spa, ensuring your complete rejuvenation.

As an indigene, I take immense pride in sharing the hidden treasures of our region, and Il San Pietro di Positano is one such gem. This legendary hotel embodies the spirit of hospitality that our people hold dear. With its private terraces overlooking the sea, sumptuous suites, and a Michelin-starred restaurant, Il San Pietro di Positano promises a truly enchanting experience.

Imagine strolling through the charming streets of Sorrento, your destination being the Grand Hotel Excelsior Vittoria. This historic masterpiece seamlessly blends modern luxury with timeless charm. From its privileged location overlooking the Bay of Naples and Mount Vesuvius to the private elevator leading to a hidden beach club, every moment spent here is imbued with coastal splendor.

Indulge in Riviera refinement at Hotel Santa Caterina, where elegance meets serenity. This family-run sanctuary captures the essence of our region, offering private terraces, a Michelin-starred restaurant, and an infinity pool that invites you to soak up the Mediterranean sun. Prepare to be embraced by the warm hospitality that has been passed down through generations.

As an indigene of the Amalfi Coast, I assure you that these luxury hotels are not just destinations; they are gateways to a world of enchantment and everlasting memories. From the iconic Le Sirenuse in Positano to the historic Palazzo Avino in Ravello, each hotel embodies the essence of our region, offering breathtaking views, sumptuous accommodations, and excellent service at the highest level

I invite you to immerse yourself in the splendor of the Amalfi Coast, where luxury seamlessly blends with our rich heritage. Let these magnificent hotels be your home away from home as you discover the timeless beauty and allure of our beloved coastal paradise.

Boutique hotel

If you seek a truly immersive and unique experience, let me introduce you to a hidden gem among the boutique hotels nestled in our beloved coastal paradise.

Picture yourself wandering through narrow cobblestone streets, surrounded by vibrant bougainvillea and the aroma of freshly baked lemon-infused treats. As an indigene of this breathtaking region, I wholeheartedly recommend the intimate and captivating La Conca Azzurra.

Nestled in the quaint village of Conca dei Marini, this boutique hotel exudes the spirit of the Amalfi Coast in every detail. As you enter, be prepared to be embraced by the warm smiles of the attentive staff, eager to make your stay truly unforgettable.

Step into your charming room, adorned with hand-painted ceramic tiles, reminiscent of our local craftsmanship. The soft sea breeze dances through the windows, inviting you to relax and savor the tranquility that surrounds you. Take a moment to unwind on your private terrace, where you can marvel at the azure waters that stretch as far as the eye can see.

Indulge in the flavors of our region at the hotel's exquisite restaurant, where local ingredients are transformed into culinary masterpieces. Feast on freshly caught seafood, aromatic herbs, and the finest ingredients our fertile land has to offer. Let the talented chefs take you on a gastronomic journey that showcases the essence of Amalfi Coast cuisine.

For a truly unforgettable experience, venture down to the hotel's private beach. Nestled in a secluded cove, this hidden oasis offers a chance to bask in the Mediterranean sun while the crystal-clear waters gently kiss the shore. Immerse yourself in the tranquility of the sea, or embark on a leisurely boat excursion to explore the nearby grottos and hidden beaches.

At La Conca Azzurra, you will not only experience the beauty of the Amalfi Coast but also connect with the genuine hospitality and warmth of our local culture. Our staff will guide you to lesser-known gems and secret spots, ensuring you uncover the true essence of our beloved coastline.

I invite you to discover the intimate charm, breathtaking views, and authentic experiences that await you at La Conca Azzurra. Let this boutique hotel become your home away from home, where cherished memories are made, and the heart of our vibrant coastal community beats passionately.

Villa Franca (Positano): Located in the heart of Positano, this boutique hotel captures the essence of Italian elegance. With stunning sea views, stylish rooms, and a rooftop pool, Villa Franca offers a luxurious retreat in one of the Amalfi Coast's most iconic destinations.

Palazzo Murat (Positano): Housed in an 18th-century palace, this boutique hotel exudes charm and history. With its lush gardens, elegant rooms, and proximity to the beach, Palazzo Murat provides a tranquil oasis in the heart of bustling Positano.

Hotel Poseidon (Positano): Combining traditional architecture with contemporary comfort, this boutique hotel offers a warm and welcoming atmosphere. Enjoy beautiful sea views, a lush garden terrace, and easy access to the town's vibrant streets and picturesque beaches.

Il San Pietro di Positano (Positano): This legendary boutique hotel epitomizes refined luxury and exclusivity. With breathtaking views, exquisite accommodations, and world-class amenities, Il San Pietro di Positano is an unparalleled retreat on the Amalfi Coast.

Hotel Villa Cimbrone (Ravello): Nestled in the charming town of Ravello, this boutique hotel boasts historic charm and stunning views. Wander through its magnificent gardens, admire the breathtaking infinity terrace, and immerse yourself in the romantic ambiance of this exquisite property.

Casa Privata (Furore): Offering a secluded and intimate experience, this boutique hotel is perched on a cliffside with panoramic sea views. With its beautifully designed rooms, a private terrace, and a sun-kissed infinity pool, Casa Privata provides a peaceful haven away from the crowds.

Hotel Santa Caterina (Amalfi): Located in Amalfi, this family-run boutique hotel offers a mix of luxury and authentic hospitality. Admire the mesmerizing sea views, indulge in gourmet cuisine, and unwind in the hotel's infinity pool perched above the cliffs.

Hotel Raito (Vietri sul Mare): Situated in the charming town of Vietri sul Mare, this boutique hotel combines modern elegance with coastal charm. Enjoy panoramic views, spacious rooms, and a serene spa for the ultimate relaxation.

These boutique hotels in the Amalfi Coast offer a personal touch, capturing the essence of the region while providing luxurious amenities and a warm atmosphere. Immerse yourself in the beauty, culture, and hospitality of the Amalfi Coast at these enchanting accommodations.

Bed and breakfast : Imagine waking up to the aroma of freshly brewed coffee, the sound of waves caressing the shore, and the gentle melodies of our local birds welcoming a new day. Our bed and breakfasts embody the spirit of our beloved land, offering a unique blend of comfort, intimacy, and genuine hospitality. Nestled within the narrow streets of our picturesque towns, these hidden gems showcase the vibrant colors and intricate architecture that define our coastal heritage. Each bed and breakfast is lovingly curated to capture the essence of our culture, providing a true immersion into our way of life. Here, you will find beautifully adorned rooms adorned with local ceramics, handmade linens, and antique furnishings that tell the stories of generations past. Open your windows to reveal sweeping vistas of the azure Mediterranean Sea or the terraced lemon groves that perfume the air with their sweet fragrance. But it is the morning feast that truly sets our bed and breakfasts apart. Our hosts, with hearts as warm as the southern sun, prepare a delectable breakfast showcasing the bounty of our land. Savor freshly baked pastries, homemade jams bursting with the flavors of our sun-ripened fruits, and locally sourced cheeses and cured meats. As you sip on freshly squeezed orange juice, savor the taste of our legendary limoncello, crafted from the plump lemons that thrive on our sun-kissed hillsides.

Venture out from your cozy retreat, and let the Amalfi Coast enchant you. Explore the winding streets of Amalfi, marvel at the grandeur of Ravello's villas perched on cliffs, or bask in the vibrant energy of Positano. Immerse yourself in the rich history, art, and traditions that have shaped our beloved homeland for centuries. In the evenings, return to your welcoming bed and breakfast, where you are greeted with genuine smiles and heartfelt conversations. Share tales of your adventures with fellow travelers, and let the camaraderie flourish over a glass of regional wine. As the day turns to dusk, allow the gentle lullaby of the sea to serenade you into a peaceful slumber, ready to awaken to another day of Amalfi Coast enchantment.

Our bed and breakfasts on the Amalfi Coast are more than mere accommodations. They are gateways to the heart and soul of our land, offering an authentic experience that transcends ordinary travel. Come, embrace our hospitality, and create cherished memories that will forever be woven into the tapestry of your Amalfi Coast journey. Benvenuti, welcome to our home.

Here are some delightful B&B recommendations that will immerse you in the authentic beauty of this coastal paradise:

Villa Maria Luigia: Nestled amidst lemon groves and overlooking the sparkling Mediterranean, Villa Maria Luigia offers a warm and inviting atmosphere. With its comfortable rooms, panoramic terrace, and delightful homemade breakfast, this family-run B&B in Amalfi is the perfect retreat for a peaceful and rejuvenating stay.

Il Dolce Rifugio: Tucked away in the picturesque town of Positano, Il Dolce Rifugio captures the essence of a true Italian escape. With its charming rooms adorned with colorful tiles and a delightful garden terrace, this B&B provides a cozy and intimate ambiance. Wake up to a delicious breakfast served with love and immerse yourself in the beauty of Positano's winding streets.

La Moresca: Located in the heart of the vibrant town of Vietri sul Mare, La Moresca offers a delightful combination of modern comforts and traditional touches. The rooms are elegantly decorated with handmade ceramics, and the panoramic terrace provides breathtaking views of the coast. Enjoy a scrumptious breakfast while soaking in the beauty of this charming B&B.

Villa Piedimonte: Situated in Ravello, known for its artistic heritage and breathtaking views, Villa Piedimonte offers a serene and tranquil atmosphere. Surrounded by lush gardens, this B&B features comfortable rooms with balconies or terraces that offer sweeping vistas. Start your day with a delightful breakfast and explore the historic treasures of Ravello at your leisure.

Casa Angelina: Perched on a cliff in Praiano, Casa Angelina combines contemporary design with breathtaking views of the Amalfi Coast. This stylish B&B offers elegant rooms, a rooftop terrace, and a delicious breakfast showcasing local flavors. Unwind in the infinity pool overlooking the sea or take a leisurely stroll to nearby beaches for a truly unforgettable experience.

Immerse yourself in the charm of the Amalfi Coast by choosing one of these delightful bed and breakfasts. Each one offers a unique blend of comfort, warm hospitality, and a chance to experience the authentic beauty of this captivating destination.

Agriturismi

Here are our top recommendations for agriturismi in the Amalfi Coast:

Villa Maria Luigia: Nestled amidst lemon and olive groves in the quaint town of Minori, Villa Maria Luigia offers a delightful agriturismo experience. Enjoy comfortable rooms with rustic charm, homegrown produce, and homemade Limoncello. Revel in the tranquility of the surrounding gardens and savor traditional dishes made with love and fresh ingredients.

Agriturismo Sant'Alfonso: Located in the lush hills of Furore, Agriturismo Sant'Alfonso provides a serene escape from the bustling coastal towns. This family-run estate offers cozy accommodations, a working farm, and breathtaking views of the Amalfi Coast. Delight your taste buds with farm-to-table meals, featuring organic vegetables, homemade cheeses, and regional specialties.

Agriturismo Il Tramonto: Situated in the scenic village of Conca dei Marini, Agriturismo Il Tramonto offers a charming retreat overlooking the Mediterranean Sea. Relax in comfortable rooms adorned with traditional furnishings and relish the warm hospitality of the hosts. Indulge in farm-fresh cuisine, with ingredients sourced from the agriturismo's own gardens and nearby farms.

Agriturismo Villa Maria: Discover a hidden oasis in the heart of Ravello at Agriturismo Villa Maria. Surrounded by terraced gardens and vineyards, this enchanting property boasts breathtaking views and a peaceful ambiance. Experience the simplicity of rural life while enjoying modern comforts, and savor traditional dishes prepared with organic ingredients from the on-site garden.

Agriturismo Il Rifugio: Find solace and tranquility at Agriturismo Il Rifugio, nestled in the picturesque village of Scala. This charming agriturismo offers cozy rooms, a welcoming atmosphere, and panoramic views of the Amalfi Coast. Taste the flavors of the land with farm-to-table meals, accompanied by local wines, and unwind amidst the beauty of nature.

Escape the ordinary and immerse yourself in the authentic charm of the Amalfi Coast with a stay at one of these delightful agriturismi. Embrace the slower pace of life, indulge in traditional cuisine, and create memories that will truly connect you to the heart and soul of this captivating region.

Chapter 4: Places for sightseeing

Town

Embark on a captivating journey along the Amalfi Coast, where every town is a treasure waiting to be discovered. Prepare to be enchanted as we unveil the best towns for sightseeing, each offering its own unique charm, history, and breathtaking views:

Positano: Nestled like a gem between cliffs and the azure sea, Positano is a town that epitomizes beauty. Explore its narrow, winding streets adorned with vibrant bougainvillea and discover picturesque squares, artisan boutiques, and quaint cafés. Don't miss the magnificent Church of Santa Maria Assunta, perched majestically overlooking the town, or the panoramic views from the Path of the Gods. Every corner of Positano is a sight to behold.

Amalfi: Immerse yourself in history and culture in the town that gave its name to the entire coast.

Amalfi boasts a rich maritime heritage and is home to the iconic Amalfi Cathedral, with its striking Arab-Norman architecture. Stroll through the charming Piazza del Duomo and explore the maze-like streets lined with boutiques selling locally made ceramics and limoncello. Take a moment to relax in the tranquil Cloister of Paradise, a hidden gem within the town.

Ravello: Perched high above the coast, Ravello offers a peaceful oasis with awe-inspiring panoramic views. Visit the famous Villa Cimbrone and its stunning gardens, where you can gaze out over the endless horizon. The architectural masterpiece of Villa Rufolo is another must-see, with its elegant gardens and magnificent backdrop. Ravello's charming streets are filled with art galleries and quaint cafés, perfect for a leisurely stroll.

Sorrento: While technically not part of the Amalfi Coast, Sorrento serves as an excellent base for exploring the region. The town is renowned for its picturesque historic center, where you can wander through charming alleyways and visit the beautiful Piazza Tasso. Enjoy stunning views of Mount Vesuvius and the Bay of Naples from the cliffs, and be sure to sample the famous limoncello, made from locally grown lemons.

Vietri sul Mare: Known as the gateway to the Amalfi Coast, Vietri sul Mare is a vibrant town renowned for its ceramics. Take a walk along the colorful streets adorned with ceramic artworks and visit the Museo della Ceramica to learn about the town's rich artistic heritage. Don't miss the chance to relax on the beach and soak in the tranquil atmosphere.

Each town along the Amalfi Coast offers a unique and captivating experience for sightseeing. From the cliffside beauty of Positano to the historic charm of Amalfi and the cultural oasis of Ravello, prepare to be enthralled by the sheer beauty and magic that this coastal paradise has to offer.

Beaches on Amalfi Coast

The Amalfi Coast is renowned for its dramatic cliffs, crystal-clear waters, and enchanting coastal villages. While it's true that the region is famous for its picturesque beaches, it's important to note that most of the beaches along the coast are pebbly rather than sandy. Nevertheless, these breathtaking coastal gems offer unparalleled beauty and are perfect for sightseeing. Here are the best beaches on the Amalfi Coast that will leave you in awe:

Fiordo di Furore: Tucked away in a hidden fjord, Fiordo di Furore is a natural wonder that should not be missed. With its steep cliffs and emerald-green waters, this secluded beach offers a truly mesmerizing sight. Take in the dramatic landscape, capture stunning photographs, and marvel at the contrast between the vibrant colors of the sea and the rugged cliffs.

Marina di Praia: Located near the village of Praiano, Marina di Praia is a charming fishing village with a small pebble beach. Surrounded by colorful houses and fishing boats, it exudes a rustic charm that is hard to resist. Enjoy a leisurely stroll along the promenade, soak up the atmosphere, and admire the picturesque scenery that this quaint beach offers.

Spiaggia Grande, Positano: Positano's Spiaggia Grande is one of the most iconic beaches on the Amalfi Coast. Nestled at the foot of the vibrant village, this pebbly beach is framed by colorful umbrellas and offers stunning views of the town's pastel-colored buildings. Bask in the sunshine, savor a refreshing drink at one of the beachfront cafés, and relish the vibrant atmosphere of this world-famous beach.

Atrani Beach: Atrani, the smallest town in Italy, is home to a lovely beach that captures the essence of the Amalfi Coast. The beach is situated in a cozy bay, framed by traditional houses and a charming piazza. Immerse yourself in the local atmosphere, admire the colorful umbrellas lining the shore, and witness the authentic coastal life that unfolds before your eyes.

Marina di Vietri: Located near Vietri sul Mare, Marina di Vietri offers a unique sightseeing experience. Known for its stunning ceramic-tiled beach, this stretch of coastline showcases the region's traditional craftsmanship. As you relax on the pebbles, marvel at the intricate designs that adorn the beach, and appreciate the artistry that has been passed down through generations.

While the Amalfi Coast may not be known for its sandy beaches, its picturesque coastal gems offer a different kind of beauty. From the rugged cliffs of Fiordo di Furore to the colorful charm of Positano's Spiaggia Grande, each beach is a sight to behold. So, embrace the pebbles, soak up the scenery, and let the captivating beauty of the Amalfi Coast leave an indelible mark on your heart.

Historic sites of Amalfi

Prepare to embark on a captivating journey through time as you explore the rich historic sites of the Amalfi Coast. Steeped in ancient lore, architectural marvels, and cultural treasures, this remarkable coastline is a treasure trove of history waiting to be discovered. Here are some of the best historic sites for sightseeing along the Amalfi Coast:

Amalfi Cathedral (Cattedrale di Sant'Andrea): Immerse yourself in the architectural splendor of the Amalfi Cathedral, located in the heart of Amalfi town. This 9th-century masterpiece showcases a harmonious blend of Byzantine, Arab, and Norman influences. Marvel at the intricate mosaics, bronze doors, and the grand staircase leading to the cathedral's stunning interior.

Villa Rufolo: Step into a world of enchantment at Villa Rufolo in Ravello. This 13th-century villa boasts stunning Moorish-influenced architecture, lush gardens, and panoramic views of the coast.

Discover the medieval tower, the impressive cloister, and the mesmerizing Terrazza dell'Infinito (Terrace of Infinity), which inspired many artists and writers.

Pompeii: While not directly on the Amalfi Coast, a visit to the ancient city of Pompeii is an absolute must. Buried under volcanic ash in 79 AD, this incredibly preserved archaeological site offers a glimpse into daily life during the Roman Empire. Explore the ruins of houses, temples, amphitheaters, and the haunting plaster casts of the victims.

Paestum: Venture south of the Amalfi Coast to the ancient Greek city of Paestum. This UNESCO World Heritage Site houses some of the best-preserved Greek temples in the world. Admire the majestic Temple of Hera, the iconic Temple of Poseidon (Neptune), and the Temple of Ceres (Athena), which transport you back to the days of Magna Graecia.

Torre dello Ziro: Discover a hidden gem in the charming village of Conca dei Marini. The Torre dello Ziro is a medieval watchtower perched on a cliff overlooking the Tyrrhenian Sea. Take in the panoramic views and imagine the tower's historic role in safeguarding the coast from invasions. It's a picturesque spot that offers a unique perspective on the region's past.

As you explore these historic sites along the Amalfi Coast, you'll be transported through centuries of history, marveling at the architectural wonders, ancient ruins, and the captivating stories that echo through time. Let the allure of the past guide your footsteps and deepen your appreciation for this remarkable region.

Garden in the Amalfi Coast

Nestled along the sun-kissed cliffs of the Amalfi Coast, a tapestry of vibrant gardens awaits to enchant your senses. Amidst the captivating beauty of this coastal paradise, the gardens of the Amalfi Coast beckon with their lush foliage, vibrant blooms, and a symphony of fragrances. Step into a world where nature's artistry reigns supreme, and let us transport you to the wondrous gardens of this mesmerizing destination.

Botanical Marvels of Ravello: Enter a realm of botanical wonder in the stunning gardens of Ravello. The Villa Cimbrone Gardens, with its meticulously manicured hedges, ornate sculptures, and breathtaking vistas, evoke a sense of timeless beauty. Lose yourself in the aromatic Lemon Grove, where the citrus-scented air and vibrant yellow fruits create an enchanting ambiance. As you stroll along the Terrace of Infinity, be captivated by the panoramic views that stretch out over the azure sea.

Tranquility Amidst Positano: Discover a serene oasis amidst the lively streets of Positano at the elegant gardens of Villa Rufolo. Immerse yourself in a symphony of colors as you wander through the terraced gardens adorned with blooming flowers, cascading fountains, and ancient architectural ruins. Unwind in the peaceful cloister garden, where the scent of citrus and the gentle sound of trickling water create a tranquil atmosphere that lingers in your memory.

Majestic Coastal Retreat in Amalfi: The Cloister of Paradise in Amalfi is a hidden gem that unveils its botanical wonders to the lucky few who venture inside. Step through the ancient arches and find yourself in a garden paradise, where lush greenery, fragrant blossoms, and an air of serenity transport you to another world. Take a moment to relax on a bench beneath the shade of towering palms, marvel at the vibrant bougainvillea, and allow the gentle breeze to carry your worries away.

Secret Gardens of Capri: Embark on a voyage to the idyllic island of Capri and discover its secret gardens that hide amidst the rugged cliffs. Explore the Gardens of Augustus, where colorful flower beds line the paths, providing exquisite views of the famous Faraglioni rock formations. As you wander through this botanical masterpiece, inhale the sweet scent of wisteria and admire the vibrant blooms of geraniums, dahlias, and bougainvillea.

Enchanting Nature in Minori: Escape the crowds and immerse yourself in the serenity of the gardens in Minori. Visit the Villa Romana, where Roman ruins and an enchanting Mediterranean garden blend harmoniously. Stroll through the terraced grounds, adorned with lemon trees, fragrant herbs, and vibrant flowers. Allow the tranquility of this hidden gem to rejuvenate your soul and create a lasting connection to the natural beauty of the Amalfi Coast.

Indulge your senses in the breathtaking gardens that grace the Amalfi Coast. Lose yourself in their captivating allure, allowing nature's splendor to uplift your spirit and ignite your imagination. These magnificent gardens are a testament to the region's rich cultural heritage and the timeless beauty that continues to captivate visitors from around the world.

Chapter 5: Food and drinks

Salve e benvenuti alla Costiera Amalfitana! I am delighted to immerse you in the exquisite culinary realm of this captivating coastal region. Nestled along the enchanting shores of southern Italy, the Amalfi Coast is renowned for its breathtaking landscapes, rich heritage, and, of course, its remarkable food and drinks.

When it comes to gastronomy, the Amalfi Coast boasts a vibrant tapestry of flavors, blending traditional Mediterranean ingredients with local produce, seafood, and age-old cooking techniques. Allow me to guide you through a delectable journey across the region's culinary treasures.

Let's begin with the cornerstone of Amalfi Coast cuisine: the lemons. Known as "sfusato amalfitano," these bright and aromatic fruits are synonymous with the region. The lemons grown in terraced gardens along the steep cliffs are revered for their exceptional quality and distinctive flavor. They find their way into countless dishes, adding a zesty touch to seafood, salads, pasta, and even desserts like the famed "delizia al limone" (lemon delight cake).

Seafood takes center stage in the Amalfi Coast's culinary repertoire, celebrating the abundant treasures of the Tyrrhenian Sea. Locally caught fish, including anchovies, sardines, red mullet, and swordfish, grace the tables in various preparations. From the simple and delicate "frittura di paranza" (mixed fried fish) to the exquisite "scialatielli ai frutti di mare" (fresh pasta with mixed seafood), every bite evokes the coastal breeze and the briny essence of the sea.

Moving on to pasta, the Amalfi Coast boasts its own unique shapes and flavors. The region's signature pasta, "scialatielli," is a thick, short pasta that pairs exquisitely with seafood, as well as with hearty meat-based sauces. Another regional specialty is "ndunderi," delicious dumplings made from ricotta cheese and served with a rich tomato sauce or delicate pesto.

As we explore further, we encounter the enticing allure of local cheeses. One cannot resist the creamy and tangy "ricotta di bufala" (buffalo ricotta) or the aged "provola del monaco," a smoked cheese with a distinctive flavor that lingers on the palate. These cheeses, accompanied by a selection of cured meats like "prosciutto di maiale nero" (black pig prosciutto), offer a delightful taste of the Amalfi Coast's pastoral traditions.

No culinary journey in this region would be complete without indulging in the traditional liqueur known as "limoncello." Crafted from the zest of Amalfi lemons, this vibrant and refreshing digestif captures the essence of the land. Savoring a chilled limoncello after a satisfying meal is a cherished tradition, providing a blissful respite as you bask in the coastal beauty.

To complement these culinary delights, the Amalfi Coast offers a rich selection of local wines. The region's viticulture thrives on steep terraced vineyards, producing unique varietals that reflect the terroir. From the crisp and citrusy white wines, such as "Furore Bianco" and "Costa d'Amalfi Bianco," to the full-bodied and robust reds like

"Tramonti Rosso" and "Tintore Costa d'Amalfi," each sip carries the essence of the sun-drenched vineyards and the maritime influence.

In addition to its renowned food and drinks, the Amalfi Coast prides itself on the conviviality and warmth of its people. The joy of sharing a meal with loved ones, savoring each bite, and immersing oneself in the lively atmosphere of a local trattoria or osteria is an integral part of the Amalfi Coast experience. The locals' passion for food and hospitality is contagious, creating an ambiance that invites you to slow down, savor the moment, and embrace the true essence of "la dolce vita."

While exploring the coastal towns, make sure to venture into the bustling street markets and specialty food shops. Here, you will discover an array of local treasures, from vibrant produce, sun-dried tomatoes, and aromatic herbs to jars of preserved anchovies, olives, and capers. These ingredients, brimming with authentic flavors, beckon you to create your own culinary masterpieces or enjoy them as simple yet sublime antipasti.

One cannot discuss Amalfi Coast cuisine without mentioning the region's famed pastries and desserts. Delicacies like "sfogliatella," a shell-shaped pastry filled with sweet ricotta cream, or "pastiera napoletana," a fragrant cake made with wheat, ricotta, and orange blossom water, tantalize the taste buds with their intricate flavors and textures. Paired with a steaming cup of espresso or a velvety cappuccino, these indulgent treats are the perfect finale to a memorable meal.

Beyond the traditional dishes, the Amalfi Coast embraces innovation and modern gastronomic trends, with talented chefs infusing their creativity into local cuisine. From Michelin-starred restaurants to charming family-run trattorias, you will find a diverse culinary landscape that caters to all tastes and preferences. Indulge in contemporary interpretations of traditional recipes, where the chefs expertly blend flavors and textures to create extraordinary culinary experiences.

It is important to note that the Amalfi Coast's culinary heritage is deeply rooted in sustainability and respect for the environment. Local producers and artisans embrace organic farming practices, ensuring the freshness and quality of their products. By supporting these sustainable initiatives, visitors contribute to the preservation of the region's natural beauty and culinary traditions for generations to come.

So, whether you find yourself perched on a cliffside terrace overlooking the azure waters, strolling through the charming cobblestone streets of Amalfi or Positano, or simply relishing the exquisite flavors at a local trattoria, the Amalfi Coast promises a gastronomic adventure like no other. It is a sensory journey that transcends mere sustenance, captivating your heart, soul, and taste buds in a symphony of flavors, aromas, and the warm embrace of Italian hospitality. Buon appetito!

Cafe and Restaurant

Allow me to guide you through the captivating cafes and restaurants that dot this stunning coastline, where gastronomic delights await.

La Taverna dei Briganti - Nestled in the heart of Amalfi, La Taverna dei Briganti offers a cozy and authentic dining experience. This rustic restaurant exudes charm with its stone walls, wooden beams, and traditional decor. Indulge in classic Italian dishes like homemade pasta, fresh seafood, and flavorful local specialties while savoring the warm ambiance. With its prime location in Amalfi, this restaurant allows you to immerse yourself in the vibrant atmosphere of the town.

Ristorante Da Gemma - Praiano Perched on a cliffside in the quaint village of Praiano, Ristorante Da Gemma offers breathtaking views of the Tyrrhenian Sea. This family-run restaurant has been serving exquisite Mediterranean cuisine for generations. Delight in their seafood delicacies, such as grilled octopus or linguine with clams, prepared with the freshest ingredients sourced from the local waters. The terrace provides a romantic setting to enjoy a candlelit dinner while marveling at the mesmerizing sunset.

Cumpa' Cosimo - Ravello Tucked away in the charming hilltop town of Ravello, Cumpa Cosimo is a culinary gem that showcases the flavors of traditional Amalfi Coast cuisine. This historic restaurant has a rich heritage and is known for its warm hospitality. Indulge in dishes like scialatielli pasta with fresh tomatoes and basil, or try their famous pollo al mattone (brick-pressed chicken) cooked to perfection. The traditional decor and panoramic views of the coastline create an inviting atmosphere.

Le Sirenuse - Positano Located within the luxurious hotel of the same name, Le Sirenuse offers an elegant and refined dining experience in the heart of Positano. The Michelin-starred restaurant presents a menu that combines Italian and international influences, showcasing the finest local ingredients. Delight in delectable dishes such as seafood risotto, roasted lamb, or delicate pastries prepared by skilled chefs. The breathtaking views of Positano's colorful houses and the glittering sea add to the overall enchantment.

Caffè Positano - Positano For a delightful break from exploring Positano's narrow streets and vibrant boutiques, Caffè Positano is the perfect spot. This charming cafe is located on the main square, where you can relax on the outdoor terrace and soak in the bustling atmosphere. Sip on a refreshing limoncello spritz or indulge in a creamy gelato while enjoying panoramic views of the town and the stunning coastline. The cafe also offers a variety of light bites, pastries, and espresso to satisfy your cravings.

Trattoria da Lorenzo - Maiori In the lesser-known town of Maiori, Trattoria da Lorenzo offers an authentic and family-friendly dining experience. This cozy trattoria specializes in traditional Italian comfort food, with an emphasis on fresh seafood and homemade pasta. Feast on the catch of the day, accompanied by a glass of local wine, and savor the flavors of the Mediterranean. The warm and welcoming atmosphere, combined with the restaurant's central location, makes it a favorite among both locals and visitors.

Il **Ritrovo - Montepertuso**

Nestled high above Positano in the village of Montepertuso, Il Ritrovo is a hidden gem worth seeking out. This charming restaurant offers panoramic views of the coastline, complemented by a menu that celebrates the rich flavors of the region. Feast on traditional dishes such as gnocchi alla Sorrentina or grilled local fish, expertly prepared using locally sourced ingredients. The warm and inviting atmosphere, along with the friendly staff, creates an unforgettable dining experience.

Ristorante Marina Grande - Ristorante Marina Grande is a popular choice for seafood enthusiasts. With a prime location just steps away from the sparkling sea, you can savor the catch of the day while enjoying stunning views. Indulge in their seafood antipasti, featuring delicacies like marinated anchovies and fresh octopus salad, followed by a main course of grilled fish or pasta with clams. The restaurant's beachside setting adds a touch of seaside charm to your dining experience.

Da Adolfo - Laurito Beach

For a truly unique dining experience, make your way to Laurito Beach, accessible by boat from Positano. Here you will find Da Adolfo, a rustic beachfront restaurant known for its relaxed atmosphere and delicious seafood. This hidden gem serves up fresh catch from the sea, prepared simply and beautifully. Try their famous spaghetti alle vongole (clam spaghetti) or indulge in grilled fish accompanied by a refreshing glass of local wine. With its idyllic setting and laid-back vibe, Da Adolfo offers a true taste of coastal bliss.

La Caravella - Amalfi

Located in a historic building in the heart of Amalfi, La Caravella is a culinary institution that has been delighting diners since 1959. Step into this elegant restaurant and be transported to a world of refined dining. The menu features a fusion of traditional Amalfi Coast flavors and international influences, with dishes like saffron-infused risotto, braised lamb shank, and mouthwatering desserts. Impeccable service and a sophisticated ambiance make La Caravella a perfect choice for a special occasion or a memorable evening out.

Il Flauto di Pan - Atrani

In the charming village of Atrani, just a short walk from Amalfi, you'll find Il Flauto di Pan, a cozy and welcoming restaurant. This family-run trattoria offers a delightful array of homemade pastas, flavorful sauces, and regional specialties. From their signature ravioli stuffed with local cheeses to the rich and comforting eggplant parmigiana, every dish is crafted with love and attention to detail. The intimate setting and friendly staff create a warm and inviting atmosphere that will make you feel right at home.

As you embark on your culinary journey along the Amalfi Coast, these cafes and restaurants beckon with their exquisite flavors, stunning vistas, and warm hospitality. Each location captures the essence of this remarkable region, where food and culture intertwine to create an unforgettable experience. Indulge in the gastronomic delights and let the Amalfi Coast cast its enchanting spell upon you.

Chapter 6: outdoor activities

Hiking: As a resident of the stunning Amalfi Coast, I am delighted to share with you the wonders of hiking in this breathtaking region. Nestled in the rugged landscape of southern Italy, the Amalfi Coast offers a multitude of hiking trails that showcase the region's natural beauty, rich history, and captivating coastal vistas. Lace up your hiking boots and prepare to embark on an unforgettable adventure through our enchanting terrain.

One of the most iconic hiking trails on the Amalfi Coast is the Path of the Gods, or "Sentiero degli Dei" in Italian. This renowned trail spans approximately 8 kilometers (5 miles) between the towns of Bomerano, near Agerola, and Nocelle, above Positano. As you traverse this ancient footpath, you will be treated to awe-inspiring panoramas of the coastline, with the azure waters of the Tyrrhenian Sea stretching out before you. The

Path of the Gods is aptly named, as you will feel like you are walking amidst the heavens, surrounded by ethereal beauty.

For a more challenging hike, consider exploring the Valle delle Ferriere, or the Valley of the Mills. This verdant valley is located near the town of Amalfi and is a designated nature reserve. As you venture deeper into the valley, you will encounter lush vegetation, cascading waterfalls, and the remnants of ancient paper mills that once thrived here. The trail meanders through the forested landscape, providing a refreshing escape from the summer heat, and culminates in a splendid waterfall known as Cascata delle Ferriere.

Another captivating hiking destination is the town of Ravello, perched high above the Amalfi Coast. From Ravello, you can embark on the trail that leads to the village of Minori, passing through terraced lemon groves and offering captivating glimpses of the coast along the way. This hike offers a unique blend of cultural and natural exploration, as you can pause to admire the exquisite gardens of Villa Cimbrone and Villa Rufolo, both known for their stunning vistas and enchanting atmosphere.

If you're up for a challenge and wish to experience the allure of Mount Vesuvius, a hike up to the crater is an absolute must. While technically not on the Amalfi Coast itself, Vesuvius is located within a short distance and offers an unforgettable adventure. The hike to the summit takes you through the volcanic landscape, providing breathtaking views of the surrounding countryside and the imposing crater at the top. Standing on the edge of Vesuvius is a humbling experience, as you can still witness the remnants of its destructive eruption in 79 AD, which famously buried the city of Pompeii.

In addition to these notable hiking trails, the Amalfi Coast boasts numerous other paths and routes that cater to all levels of hiking expertise. From leisurely strolls through picturesque villages like Positano and Atrani to more challenging treks along the Monti Lattari mountain range, there is something for everyone to enjoy. Remember to bring proper footwear, water, sunscreen, and a camera to capture the mesmerizing landscapes that unfold before your eyes.

As you explore the Amalfi Coast through hiking, you will not only witness the beauty of nature but also immerse yourself in the local culture and history. The combination of breathtaking scenery, charming towns, and ancient footpaths creates an unforgettable experience that will leave a lasting impression on your heart and soul. So come, embrace the call of the mountains and trails, and discover the true essence of the Amalfi Coast through the exhilarating adventure of hiking.

Scuba diving

Let me enchant you with tales of scuba diving, an exhilarating outdoor activity that captures the essence of our coastal paradise. Nestled along the Tyrrhenian Sea in southern Italy, the Amalfi Coast is renowned for its captivating beauty both above and below the water's surface.

Venturing into the depths of the Mediterranean Sea through scuba diving allows you to explore a vibrant underwater world teeming with marine life, ancient ruins, and hidden treasures. The crystal-clear waters that embrace our coastline are an invitation to immerse yourself in an unforgettable adventure.

The town of Amalfi, for which our beloved coastline is named, serves as an excellent starting point for scuba diving enthusiasts. From here, you can embark on thrilling dives in various locations that showcase the diversity and splendor of the Amalfi Coast's underwater realm.

One such captivating spot is the Grotta dello Smeraldo, or Emerald Grotto, located near the village of Conca dei Marini. This enchanting cavern gets its name from the mesmerizing emerald light that filters through an underwater opening, creating a magical ambiance for divers. Exploring the depths of the Emerald Grotto reveals an extraordinary display of stalactites, stalagmites, and rock formations, creating a truly ethereal experience.

Continuing westward, we arrive at the picturesque village of Positano, which serves as another gateway to underwater marvels. The waters surrounding Positano are renowned for their exceptional visibility, allowing divers to marvel at the vivid hues of marine life and the remnants of ancient civilizations.

Just off the coast of Positano lies Li Galli Islands, a group of small, rocky islets shrouded in myth and legend. These islands offer an awe-inspiring dive site, where divers can encounter vibrant schools of fish, elegant corals, and even the occasional encounter with playful dolphins.

Further along the coast, we reach the charming town of Praiano, which offers access to another remarkable dive site known as the Punta Campanella Marine Reserve. This protected area is a haven for underwater biodiversity, showcasing an abundance of colorful fish species, intricate coral formations, and impressive underwater caves waiting to be explored.

Lastly, the town of Maiori beckons adventurers with its underwater wonders. Here, you can delve into the depths of the ancient Roman villa submerged in the sea, known as Villa Romana. This archeological marvel transports divers back in time, allowing them to marvel at the remnants of an opulent past amidst the enchanting marine environment.

Whether you are a seasoned diver or a curious novice, the Amalfi Coast offers an array of scuba diving experiences that will leave you in awe. Dive into the azure waters, explore hidden treasures, and be captivated by the rich biodiversity that thrives beneath the surface. As an indigene of this coastal paradise, I can assure you that scuba diving along the Amalfi Coast is an adventure you will treasure forever.

Kayaking

I am thrilled to share with you the wonders of kayaking, one of the most exhilarating outdoor activities you can experience in our breathtaking region. Nestled along the stunning coastline of southern Italy, the Amalfi Coast offers a plethora of hidden coves, pristine beaches, and azure waters that are perfect for exploring by kayak.

One of the most popular locations for kayaking along the Amalfi Coast is the enchanting town of Amalfi itself. With its rich history, charming architecture, and vibrant atmosphere, Amalfi serves as an ideal starting point for your kayaking adventure. You can rent a kayak from one of the local outfitters and embark on a journey along the coastline, witnessing the stunning cliffs, ancient watchtowers, and picturesque villages that dot the landscape.

Just a short distance east of Amalfi lies the captivating village of Atrani. Known for its narrow streets and colorful houses, Atrani offers a unique kayaking experience. Glide along the coastline and marvel at the contrast between the vibrant architecture and the deep blue sea. Paddle past the Torre dello Ziro, an ancient fortress perched atop a cliff, and enjoy the tranquility of the surroundings as you immerse yourself in the beauty of nature.

For those seeking a more secluded and serene kayaking experience, the secluded bay of Conca dei Marini is an excellent choice. Located between Amalfi and Praiano, this hidden gem boasts crystal-clear waters and towering cliffs that provide a sense of isolation and tranquility. As you paddle through the calm waters, you'll have the opportunity to explore hidden sea caves, such as the enchanting Grotta dello Smeraldo (Emerald Grotto), known for its mesmerizing emerald-green reflections.

Continuing westward, the charming town of Positano beckons kayakers with its iconic pastel-colored houses cascading down the cliffs. From here, you can set off on a kayaking adventure towards the striking Li Galli Islands. These small archipelagos are steeped in mythology and are said to have been inhabited by the mythical sirens who enticed sailors with their enchanting songs. As you paddle around the islands, take in the breathtaking views of the rugged coastline and immerse yourself in the mythical allure of the region.

Finally, no kayaking experience along the Amalfi Coast would be complete without a visit to the picturesque town of Sorrento. Situated on a cliff overlooking the Bay of Naples, Sorrento offers a fantastic starting point for exploring the neighboring isle of Capri by kayak. Enjoy the calm waters as you paddle past the iconic Faraglioni rock formations and venture into hidden sea caves, such as the enchanting Blue Grotto, renowned for its mesmerizing azure glow.

Kayaking along the Amalfi Coast is an adventure that allows you to immerse yourself in the beauty of this UNESCO World Heritage site. From the charming streets of Amalfi to the secluded bays of Conca dei Marini and the mythical islands near Positano, each location offers a unique experience that showcases the region's natural splendor. So, grab a paddle, embrace the tranquility of the sea, and let the wonders of the Amalfi Coast unfold before you as you embark on an unforgettable kayaking journey.

Paragliding

Nestled along the rugged cliffs and overlooking the sparkling turquoise waters of the Tyrrhenian Sea, the Amalfi Coast offers a truly magical backdrop for an unforgettable paragliding adventure.

The Amalfi Coast boasts several prime locations for paragliding, each offering its own unique charm and panoramic views. Let's explore some of the most popular spots that will make your paragliding experience truly remarkable.

Ravello: Known for its enchanting beauty and stunning coastal vistas, Ravello is a charming hilltop town that provides an ideal launching point for paragliding. Imagine soaring high above the town's iconic villas and lush gardens, with the Amalfi Coast stretching out below you like a vibrant mosaic of colors.

Positano: Renowned for its picturesque cliffside village, Positano offers a remarkable paragliding experience. After ascending into the sky, you'll witness the terraced buildings and pastel-colored houses cascading down to the sparkling waters. The view of Positano from above is simply awe-inspiring and will surely leave you breathless.

Amalfi: Steeped in history and charm, the town of Amalfi is another excellent location for paragliding enthusiasts. As you glide through the air, you'll have a bird's-eye view of the town's impressive cathedral, vibrant squares, and the labyrinthine streets that wind their way towards the sea. The sight of the emerald green waters meeting the rugged coastline is a sight you'll cherish forever.

Praiano: Nestled between Positano and Amalfi, Praiano is a hidden gem that offers a more tranquil paragliding experience. The serene atmosphere and panoramic views of the Amalfi Coast from above create an incredible sense of freedom and serenity. Prepare to be captivated by the pristine beaches, colorful fishing boats, and the majestic cliffs that define this lesser-known destination.

Scala: If you're seeking a paragliding adventure that combines adrenaline and serenity, look no further than Scala. This peaceful hillside town offers stunning views of the Amalfi Coast, with its terraced gardens and olive groves stretching as far as the eye can see. Soar high above Scala and revel in the tranquility of the surrounding countryside.

It's worth noting that paragliding in the Amalfi Coast is a weather-dependent activity, and it's essential to consult with local paragliding operators and experienced pilots to ensure safe and enjoyable flights. These professionals will guide you through the necessary preparations and provide the required equipment.

Whether you're an experienced paraglider or a beginner looking for an adventure of a lifetime, the Amalfi Coast offers a diverse range of locations that will take your breath away. Soar through the sky, embrace the wind, and witness the unparalleled beauty of this Mediterranean paradise. Paragliding on the Amalfi Coast is an experience that will forever remain etched in your heart and soul

Chapter 7: Shopping Experience

Famous Markets

Embark on a delightful shopping journey as we explore the famous markets that grace this breathtaking coastline. From the bustling streets of Amalfi to the charming villages of Positano and Ravello, these markets offer a treasure trove of local delights, handmade crafts, and delectable treats.

Let's begin our exploration in the heart of the Amalfi town itself, where the Piazza del Duomo market unfolds like a picturesque scene from a storybook. Located just steps away from the magnificent Cathedral of Amalfi, this market is a haven for avid shoppers and culture enthusiasts. Stroll through the maze of narrow lanes lined with quaint stalls selling a myriad of goods. Discover intricate handcrafted ceramics, exquisite

Limoncello liqueur, and delightful local delicacies such as sfogliatelle and pastiera, traditional pastries that will tantalize your taste buds. Immerse yourself in the lively atmosphere as vendors engage in friendly banter, their voices blending with the melodious chimes of the nearby clock tower.

A short drive along the winding coastal road brings us to the vibrant village of Positano, famous for its colorful cliffside houses and picturesque beaches. Here, the market at Piazza dei Mulini is a visual feast for the senses. As you meander through the streets, you'll encounter an array of elegant boutiques and artisan shops showcasing Positano's renowned fashion and handmade sandals. Lose yourself in the vibrant hues of the iconic Positano style, characterized by flowy fabrics, intricate embroidery, and sun-kissed patterns. Take a moment to savor the aroma of freshly brewed coffee wafting from the local cafes as you admire the magnificent view of the Tyrrhenian Sea.

Our journey now takes us to the charming hilltop village of Ravello, perched high above the coastline and renowned for its cultural heritage. In the heart of Ravello, you'll find the bustling weekly market at Piazza Duomo, where locals and visitors converge to experience its authentic charm. Marvel at the abundance of fresh produce and local specialties, including the region's celebrated buffalo mozzarella, juicy tomatoes, and fragrant lemons. Delight in the intricate lacework and embroidery adorning the stalls, a testament to Ravello's rich artistic traditions. As you explore the market, soak in the panoramic views of the sparkling azure sea and the verdant hills that surround this captivating village.

Beyond these three iconic markets, the Amalfi Coast is also dotted with smaller, hidden gems that offer a more intimate shopping experience. From the artisan workshops in the village of Atrani, where master craftsmen breathe life into hand-carved cameos and intricate silver jewelry, to the farmer's market in Maiori, where you can sample an array of locally grown fruits and vegetables, each market adds its unique touch to the vibrant tapestry of this coastal region.

The markets of the Amalfi Coast are not only a shopper's paradise but also a gateway to the region's rich cultural heritage. Embark on this journey, and you will not only return with cherished mementos but also with memories of the warm hospitality and vibrant spirit of the people who call this coastline home. So, immerse yourself in the colors, flavors, and traditions of the Amalfi Coast markets, and let the magic of this enchanting region captivate your soul.

Special Stores

As an indigenous resident of this breathtaking region, I am thrilled to guide you through the charming streets and reveal the hidden gems of our special stores. Whether you are a connoisseur of fashion, a lover of local craftsmanship, or a seeker of unique souvenirs, the Amalfi Coast offers a plethora of delightful shopping experiences.

Let us begin our journey in the picturesque town of Amalfi itself. Nestled between towering cliffs and adorned with vibrant pastel-colored buildings, Amalfi boasts an array of boutique shops. One must-visit establishment is Marina Grande, located near the main square. This elegant store showcases a curated collection of high-end fashion brands, blending Italian sophistication with coastal charm.

Moving along the coast, our next stop is the charming village of Positano. Known for its cascading white houses and narrow streets, Positano is a haven for fashion enthusiasts. One of the iconic stores here is Emporio Sirenuse. Situated on the fashionable Via del Saracino, this boutique offers a range of exquisite clothing, accessories, and home décor items, all inspired by the allure of the Mediterranean lifestyle.

Continuing our shopping adventure, we arrive at the charming town of Ravello, perched high above the coastline. Here, you will discover delightful artisanal shops specializing in ceramics, a traditional craft of the region. Ceramiche d'Arte Pascal is a renowned store, known for its beautifully hand-painted ceramics. From intricately designed tiles to colorful tableware, each piece tells a story of craftsmanship and heritage.

A short distance away lies the village of Maiori, where you can explore a hidden treasure trove of culinary delights. Step into Sal De Riso, a renowned pastry shop that has been tantalizing taste buds for generations. Indulge in delectable pastries, mouthwatering cakes, and irresistible gelato, all made with locally sourced ingredients. The scents and flavors that emanate from this store will transport you to a world of sweet bliss.

As our shopping expedition continues, we make our way to the captivating town of Sorrento. Famous for its lemon groves and limoncello liqueur, Sorrento offers an abundance of shops specializing in lemon-infused products. Limonoro is a charming boutique where you can find an array of lemon-scented candles, soaps, lotions, and, of course, the iconic limoncello. Immerse yourself in the refreshing citrus aroma that permeates this enchanting store.

Our final stop on this shopping odyssey takes us to the quaint village of Vietri sul Mare, renowned for its vibrant hand-painted ceramics. Delight in the cheerful colors and intricate designs of the ceramics at Ceramiche Vietresi. From plates and vases to tiles and decorative objects, these creations are a testament to the region's rich artistic heritage. Take a piece of this unique craftsmanship home with you as a cherished memento.

As you wander through the charming towns and immerse yourself in the local culture, these special stores of the Amalfi Coast will leave an indelible mark on your shopping experience. From high-end fashion boutiques to traditional artisanal shops, each location holds its own allure. Embrace the warmth and beauty of this coastal paradise as you explore the treasures that await you at every turn. Happy shopping.

Chapter 8: Culture and Arts

Festivals

Ah, the enchanting Amalfi Coast! A place where tradition dances with the waves and celebrations breathe life into every corner. Come, dear traveler, let me be your guide as we delve into the vibrant tapestry of festivals that grace this picturesque region.

One cannot speak of festivals in Amalfi without mentioning the grandest of them all

that grace this captivating coastal paradise.

Festival of Sant'Andrea (November 30th): The Festival of Sant'Andrea is the grandest and most revered festival in Amalfi. This religious celebration pays homage to Saint Andrew, the patron saint of Amalfi. The festivities commence with a solemn procession, where a statue of Sant'Andrea is carried through the labyrinthine streets, accompanied by the town's band. The statue is then brought to the magnificent Cathedral of Sant'Andrea, where a special Mass is held. The streets come alive with colorful decorations, traditional crafts, delectable food, and joyful revelry. The night sky lights up with a spectacular fireworks display, and music and dancing fill the air, creating an atmosphere of pure enchantment.

Festival of the Annunciation (March 25th): The Festival of the Annunciation is a joyous celebration of the announcement of the Virgin Mary's impending motherhood. The town adorns itself with vibrant floral decorations, symbolizing the arrival of spring. A procession takes place, leading to the Church of Santa Maria Assunta, where a Mass is conducted. The festival exudes a sense of renewal and new beginnings, capturing the essence of hope and faith.

Ravello Festival (Summer Months): The Ravello Festival is a world-renowned event that celebrates the arts, particularly music, in the idyllic town of Ravello. Held during the summer months, this festival attracts renowned musicians, orchestras, and artists from around the globe. Open-air concerts are held in magnificent venues such as the Villa Rufolo and Villa Cimbrone, offering breathtaking views as the backdrop to the harmonious melodies. The Ravello Festival is a true cultural extravaganza that enchants both locals and visitors alike.

Regatta of the Ancient Maritime Republics (Every four years): The Regatta of the Ancient Maritime Republics is a captivating event that celebrates Amalfi's seafaring heritage. Taking place every four years, this historic regatta brings together the ancient maritime republics of Amalfi, Pisa, Genoa, and Venice. The azure waters of the Tyrrhenian Sea become the stage for a thrilling boat race, where rowers showcase their skill and precision. Spectators line the coastline, cheering on their favorite teams, immersing themselves in the maritime spirit, and experiencing the rich history of the region.

These are just a glimpse of the festivals that grace the Amalfi Coast throughout the year. The region's deep-rooted traditions, combined with its awe-inspiring natural beauty, create a captivating atmosphere that enchants and leaves a lasting impression on all who partake in these joyous celebrations. So, immerse yourself in the vibrant festivities, embrace the local culture, and let the Amalfi Coast weave its magic upon your soul.

Art Galleries

I take great pride in the art galleries that grace our picturesque region. Nestled along the rugged cliffs and overlooking the azure waters of the Tyrrhenian Sea, Amalfi is a haven for artists, art enthusiasts, and anyone seeking inspiration in the realm of creativity.

The art galleries of Amalfi embody the essence of our rich cultural heritage and the artistic traditions that have flourished in this region for centuries. They serve as a vibrant tapestry, weaving together the threads of history, imagination, and talent, allowing visitors to immerse themselves in a world of artistic wonders.

One of the most renowned art galleries in Amalfi is the Galleria dell'Arte Amalfitana, situated in the heart of the town. This gallery showcases a remarkable collection of artwork by local artists, reflecting the diverse styles and influences that have shaped our region's artistic identity. From traditional oil paintings capturing the idyllic coastal landscapes to contemporary mixed media installations pushing the boundaries of creativity, the Galleria dell'Arte Amalfitana is a true treasure trove of artistic expression.

For those with a penchant for classical art, the Museo della Carta, or the Paper Museum, is a must-visit destination. While not solely an art gallery, this unique museum pays homage to the ancient art of papermaking, a craft that has been intertwined with the history of Amalfi since the Middle Ages. Visitors can explore the intricate process of paper production and marvel at the delicate artworks crafted from handmade paper. The museum's exhibits feature stunning paper sculptures, intricate calligraphy, and ancient manuscripts, showcasing the exceptional skill and creativity of the artisans who have kept this traditional craft alive.

Moving away from the traditional gallery setting, Amalfi also boasts a number of open-air art spaces that perfectly blend art and nature. The Giardino dell'Arte, or the Garden of Art, is a breathtaking outdoor gallery tucked away in a secluded corner of the coastline. Here, sculptures and installations emerge harmoniously from the lush Mediterranean flora, creating an enchanting environment where nature and art intertwine.

Beyond Amalfi itself, neighboring towns along the coast also offer their own art galleries, each with its unique character and charm. Positano, known for its vibrant colors and bohemian atmosphere, hosts several galleries that showcase contemporary and abstract works, reflecting the town's lively spirit. Ravello, perched high above the coastline, boasts galleries that focus on classical and Renaissance art, attracting visitors with their timeless beauty and historical significance.

Art galleries on the Amalfi Coast not only provide a platform for local artists to display their talent but also create a bridge between the past and the present. They preserve the artistic legacy of our ancestors while nurturing and inspiring future generations of artists. Whether you are an art aficionado, a curious traveler, or simply someone who appreciates beauty in all its forms, the art galleries of Amalfi Coast offer an immersive experience that will leave you captivated and inspired.

In conclusion, the art galleries of Amalfi Coast are a testament to the region's creative spirit and cultural heritage. They offer a kaleidoscope of artistic expression, ranging from traditional to contemporary, from paintings to sculptures, and from indoor galleries to outdoor installations. Exploring these galleries is an invitation to embark on a visual journey through time, history, and the boundless depths of human imagination. Come, let the art of Amalfi Coast transport you to a world where beauty knows no limits.

Music

The Amalfi Coast is renowned for its breathtaking landscapes, vibrant traditions, and rich history, and our music is a reflection of these elements.

Traditional music in Amalfi is deeply rooted in our local customs and is often characterized by its lively and infectious rhythms. One of the most famous and beloved genres is the Tarantella, a traditional Italian dance that originated in Southern Italy. The Tarantella is known for its energetic tempo, vibrant melodies, and intricate footwork. It has been passed down through generations and remains a cherished part of our cultural heritage.

In addition to the Tarantella, Amalfi is also known for its traditional folk songs, which tell stories of love, loss, and daily life. These songs are often accompanied by simple yet captivating melodies played on traditional instruments such as the guitar, mandolin, and accordion. The lyrics are typically sung in the local dialect, adding an authentic and intimate touch to the music.

The Amalfi Coast has also embraced various other genres and musical influences over the years. With its close proximity to Naples, the birthplace of renowned Italian singer-songwriters, our region has been influenced by Neapolitan music. The heartfelt and melodious tunes of Neapolitan songs have found a place in the hearts of many Amalfi Coast residents, with their emotional lyrics resonating deeply within our community.

Furthermore, Amalfi has been a source of inspiration for artists from all around the world. The stunning coastline, picturesque towns, and the tranquil sounds of the waves crashing against the cliffs have inspired numerous musicians, composers, and artists. Many have sought to capture the essence of Amalfi through their music, creating compositions that evoke the beauty and serenity of our beloved region.

Today, Amalfi continues to celebrate its musical traditions through various festivals, concerts, and cultural events. These gatherings provide a platform for local musicians and performers to showcase their talent and keep the spirit of our music alive. Whether it's a lively street performance or an intimate concert in a historic venue, the music of Amalfi brings people together, creating a sense of unity and joy.

Moreover, music plays a significant role in our daily lives, enhancing social gatherings, family celebrations, and religious ceremonies. It creates a vibrant atmosphere, encouraging everyone to join in and share the joyous moments together. From weddings and festivals to religious processions and local festivities, music infuses every aspect of our cultural identity, reflecting the passion and zest for life that defines the people of the Amalfi Coast.

In conclusion, the music of the Amalfi Coast is a testament to the region's rich cultural heritage and the profound connection we have with our surroundings. It embodies the spirit of our vibrant communities and serves as a way to express our emotions, tell our stories, and celebrate life. Whether through traditional tunes, folk songs, or contemporary compositions, music in Amalfi is a source of inspiration, unity, and boundless joy.

Chapter 9: Practical Information

Currency of Amalfi Coast

I am delighted to shed light upon the unique currency and the best places to exchange your money.

The official currency of the Amalfi Coast is the Euro (€), which is the widely accepted legal tender throughout Italy. Within the coastal towns that grace our breathtaking landscape, you will find numerous establishments, including banks, exchange offices, and authorized currency exchange booths, where you can easily convert your currency to Euros. These establishments are typically found in bustling town centers or conveniently located near popular tourist areas, ensuring accessibility for all visitors.

One such place to perform currency exchange is the Amalfi Exchange Bureau, situated at the heart of the historic Amalfi town. This reputable establishment prides itself on providing fair exchange rates and excellent service to locals and travelers alike. With their professional and friendly staff, you can confidently exchange your currency and obtain Euros for your exploration of the Amalfi Coast's wonders.

Another notable exchange point is the Positano Currency Exchange, nestled amidst the vibrant streets of Positano, a charming village that captivates all who wander its cobblestone paths. This establishment is renowned for its reliability and efficient currency conversion services. Here, you can seamlessly transform your foreign currency into Euros, ensuring you are ready to indulge in the splendor of our coastal paradise.

For those venturing towards the captivating town of Ravello, the Ravello Exchange Center offers a convenient stop to convert your money. Located near the main square, this establishment is well-regarded for its secure transactions and knowledgeable staff. Whether you seek to exchange banknotes or utilize other financial services, the Ravello Exchange Center is an excellent choice for your currency needs.

In addition to these prominent exchange centers, many local banks throughout the Amalfi Coast are equipped to facilitate currency conversions. These institutions, such as Banca di Salerno and Banca di Napoli, are trusted sources that can cater to your financial requirements efficiently.

While currency exchange options are plentiful within the Amalfi Coast, it is advisable to compare rates and transaction fees before committing to any specific establishment. This way, you can ensure the most favorable exchange rates and minimize any unnecessary charges

Safety and Health

With its stunning landscapes, captivating history, and warm-hearted locals, Amalfi Coast is a destination that will surely steal your heart. However, it is essential to prioritize your well-being while immersing yourself in the wonders of our beloved home. Allow me to share some invaluable safety tips and precautions to ensure your visit is a safe and memorable experience.

Sun Protection:

The radiant Mediterranean sun can be both delightful and fierce. Shield yourself from its rays by wearing sunscreen with a high SPF, a wide-brimmed hat, sunglasses, and lightweight clothing. Seek shade during the peak hours of the day, typically between 11 a.m. and 3 p.m., when the sun's intensity is at its peak.

Stay Hydrated:

Amalfi Coast is blessed with a warm climate, especially during the summer months. It is crucial to stay hydrated throughout the day, so remember to carry a water bottle with you. Sip water frequently to keep your body refreshed and avoid dehydration.

Safe Swimming:

Our coastline boasts crystal-clear waters that beckon for a refreshing dip. However, it is vital to swim in designated areas under the watchful eyes of lifeguards. Pay attention to safety flags and signs indicating sea conditions. Be cautious of hidden rocks and currents, especially in more secluded coves.

Cliffside Precautions:

Amalfi Coast is renowned for its awe-inspiring cliffs and panoramic vistas. While these views are breathtaking, exercise caution when exploring cliffside areas. Stay on marked paths, avoid leaning too far over edges, and keep a safe distance from unstable or crumbling cliffs.

Road Safety:

If you choose to explore the region by car or scooter, exercise extra care on the winding coastal roads. Familiarize yourself with local traffic rules, stay within speed limits, and be attentive to other drivers. Parking can be limited, so park in designated areas to avoid fines or inconvenience to other road users.

Hiking Trails:

Amalfi Coast offers splendid hiking opportunities with trails that wind through verdant hills and ancient footpaths. Before setting off, ensure you have appropriate footwear, carry a map or guidebook, and inform someone of your intended route. Take note of any closures or restrictions, especially during adverse weather conditions.

Respect Nature and Wildlife:

Amalfi Coast's natural beauty is a testament to the harmony between man and nature. Please do your part in preserving this delicate balance by respecting wildlife and ecosystems. Do not leave litter behind, avoid picking flowers or disturbing fauna, and refrain from feeding wild animals.

Local Cuisine and Hygiene:

Indulge in the rich culinary offerings of our region, but ensure you prioritize food safety and hygiene. Dine in reputable establishments, where proper food handling practices are observed. Drink bottled water, and be cautious with uncooked foods or street vendors.

Medical Assistance:

In case of any health concerns or emergencies, rest assured that Amalfi Coast has excellent medical facilities. Familiarize yourself with the location of nearby hospitals or clinics and carry essential medications or medical information with you if needed.

COVID-19 Precautions:

During these times, it is crucial to remain vigilant and follow guidelines related to COVID-19. Stay updated on local regulations, wear masks in indoor settings or crowded areas, maintain physical distance, and practice good hand hygiene.

Dear traveler, as you embark on your Amalfi Coast adventure, remember that your safety and well-being are paramount. By heeding these safety tips and precautions, you can immerse yourself in the magic of our beloved Amalfi Coast while ensuring a worry-free experience. Allow the vibrant colors of Positano, the architectural marvels of Amalfi, and the tranquil beauty of Ravello to captivate your senses, knowing that you have taken the necessary steps to safeguard your health and safety.

Immerse yourself in the warm embrace of our community, for the locals are always ready to extend a helping hand and share their boundless hospitality. Embrace the dolce vita, savor the delectable flavors of our traditional cuisine, and indulge in the serene coastal atmosphere. However, do so with a mindful approach, respecting the local customs and natural environment.

In the quaint towns and villages that dot the coastline, take leisurely strolls through the narrow cobblestone streets. Admire the centuries-old architecture, such as the grandeur of the Cathedral of Amalfi or the opulent villas that perch on the hillsides. As you explore, be cautious of uneven surfaces, especially when venturing into less touristy areas.

When venturing out on boat trips or excursions, ensure you choose reputable tour operators who prioritize safety and adhere to regulations. Life jackets should be readily available, and vessels should be well-maintained. Familiarize yourself with emergency procedures and listen carefully to instructions provided by the crew.

In crowded places, such as bustling markets or popular tourist sites, be aware of your belongings at all times. Keep valuable items secure, preferably in a concealed money belt or pouch. Vigilance and awareness will go a long way in ensuring a hassle-free experience.

While the Amalfi Coast offers a myriad of recreational activities, from kayaking to hiking, it is important to assess your own abilities and limitations. Choose activities that align with your fitness level and consult with professionals or local guides if needed. Safety should always be the priority, allowing you to fully enjoy the breathtaking landscapes and natural wonders that await you.

Lastly, embrace the spirit of adventure, but exercise caution when venturing into less-explored areas. Inform someone of your plans and estimated return time, especially when embarking on solo adventures or challenging hikes.

Dear visitor, as an indigene of the Amalfi Coast, I implore you to treat our home with the utmost respect and care. By embracing these safety tips and precautions, you will have the privilege of immersing yourself in the captivating beauty of our region while ensuring a journey that is both memorable and secure. May your time in Amalfi Coast be filled with joy, wonder, and cherished memories that will last a lifetime. Buon viaggio!

Sustainability and Responsible tourism

Our stunning coastline, with its cascading cliffs, turquoise waters, and charming towns, is a treasure that must be preserved for generations to come. In order to maintain the beauty and ecological integrity of the Amalfi Coast, it is imperative that we adopt sustainable practices and promote responsible tourism.

The Amalfi Coast is not only a tourist destination but also our home. We have a profound connection with the natural environment that surrounds us, and we recognize the importance of preserving it. Sustainability lies at the core of our values, and we strive to find a balance between tourism and environmental conservation.

One of the key aspects of responsible tourism is minimizing our impact on the delicate ecosystem of the Amalfi Coast. This begins with the responsible use of resources. As residents and visitors, we should be mindful of our water consumption, energy usage, and waste management. Simple actions such as using water sparingly, turning off lights and air conditioning when not needed, and properly recycling can make a significant difference.

Furthermore, it is crucial to support local businesses and artisans who embrace sustainable practices. By choosing locally sourced products and services, we can reduce the carbon footprint associated with transportation and contribute to the economic development of our communities. From enjoying traditional cuisine made with locally grown ingredients to purchasing handmade crafts from local artisans, we can foster a sustainable economy that celebrates our rich cultural heritage.

Preserving the natural beauty of the Amalfi Coast also entails protecting its fragile ecosystems. The coastal region is home to a diverse array of flora and fauna, and it is our responsibility to safeguard their habitats. We must respect protected areas and wildlife reserves, refraining from disturbing the natural balance. Responsible tourism also means engaging in activities that have a minimal impact on the environment, such as hiking, kayaking, or exploring on foot rather than relying solely on motorized vehicles.

In order to promote sustainability and responsible tourism, education and awareness are paramount. Local authorities, community organizations, and tourism agencies should collaborate to educate visitors about the fragility of the ecosystem and the importance of preserving it. Informative signage, guided tours, and interactive experiences can all play a role in raising awareness and promoting responsible behavior.

Furthermore, implementing strict regulations and guidelines for tourism activities can help ensure sustainable practices. Limiting the number of visitors to sensitive areas, controlling the construction of new infrastructure, and enforcing sustainable fishing practices are just a few examples of the measures that can be taken to protect the Amalfi Coast.

By embracing sustainability and responsible tourism, we can preserve the Amalfi Coast's natural beauty, support our local communities, and create a thriving environment for both residents and visitors. Let us cherish this extraordinary destination and work together to safeguard its ecological integrity for future generations to enjoy.

Conclusion

From its breathtaking cliffs and vibrant turquoise waters to its charming towns and delectable cuisine, this coastal gem offers an unparalleled experience that truly embodies the essence of la dolce vita.

Whether you seek relaxation, adventure, or a taste of the rich Italian culture, the Amalfi Coast has it all. Lose yourself in the maze-like streets of Positano, bask in the beauty of Ravello's gardens, or embark on a scenic hike along the Path of the Gods. Indulge in exquisite seafood, sample limoncello made from the region's famous lemons, and savor every moment of la dolce vita.

But beyond its physical allure, the Amalfi Coast is a place that touches the soul. It's a destination that evokes a sense of wonder and inspires a deep appreciation for the beauty that exists in the world. Whether you're gazing at the sunset from a cliffside terrace, exploring hidden coves by boat, or simply strolling along the coastline, the Amalfi Coast invites you to embrace life's simple pleasures and celebrate the joy of living.

So, let the Amalfi Coast weave its magic around you. Immerse yourself in its timeless beauty, let its vibrant colors ignite your imagination, and allow its warm hospitality to envelop you. Whether you're a seasoned traveler or embarking on your first adventure, the Amalfi Coast promises an experience that will stay with you forever.

In the end, the Amalfi Coast isn't just a destination—it's a journey of the heart. So pack your bags, set sail along the coast, and let the Amalfi Coast be the backdrop to your own unforgettable story.

Manufactured by Amazon.ca
Acheson, AB